A WOMAN WITH SEVERAL LIVES

A WOMAN WITH SEVERAL LIVES

Jean Daive
TRANSLATION BY Norma Cole

LA PRESSE   IOWA CITY & PARIS   2012

Une femme de quelques vies copyright © 2009 Flammarion
Translation copyright © 2012 Norma Cole

Published in the United States by La Presse,
an imprint of Fence Books

La Presse/Fence Books are distributed by Consortium
www.cbsd.com
www.lapressepoetry.com

Library of Congress Control Number 2011929377
Daive, Jean
A Woman with Several Lives by Jean Daive,
translated by Norma Cole
p.   cm.

ISBN 978-1-934200-51-3

1. French poetry. 2. Poetry. 3. Contemporary translation.

First Edition
10 9 8 7 6 5 4 3 2 1

We would like to thank Flammarion, who first published this book in
French in 2009, and we'd especially like to thank Yves di Mano, the
editor of their contemporary poetry series, and the author himself
for graciously granting us permission to publish this translation.

FIRST NOTEBOOK

All the children are swaddled

as white
as
dried beans
sheltered from the air

for time
even recycles
pots
of jam

Indian graves
at lake
Koshkonong

and upon this memory

a ball rolls
up to the sacred
excavations.

The golfers
play
among the corpses.

The oath is not more
newsworthy

than the government
of words
around the table

a Sunday
at home.

Everything keeps
a smell of milk
and clean house.

What is the role
of the water
pump

in a peaceful day?

It's raining
The wind rises.

The river
softer

than the rain
falling
on the roof

lights up.

Water is everywhere
outside.

The window.
Always.

And what it shows
in a reduced space.

Couch.
Chair and table.

Bed. Floor.

Stove.

Enameled oven.

The memories are there
along the river
that moves on.

The window opposite
lights up the same objects

but in inverse order.

Space forms a square.
Four angles.

Grass is airy and

the trees –
                witnesses

A wild
bank retained
by stones.

Trunks. Branches.

Grass and pink
mushrooms.

The clouds are very low.

The pump has
certainly
captured History.

The radiator
bad weather.

This field in front of the landing
is very damp.

Dispossession

since it's natural
to flow

has value of nocturnal
transfers
of exchanges.

Children
well replace
trees.

How to talk about
bodies and
organs

before so much
nature

under the surveillance
of the water.

Water takes the place
is the place

of all directed
logic.

Water slides off the roof.

Just one big
cloud
sitting on the range
of gold buttons

And the rain is falling
in the ditch
that sets the stones.

The weather is
white.

The hours are
white.

Smell of damp
woods.

Decay
revealed by the mushrooms.

Smell of oil
and gas mixed with soil.

It is a garage
closed for 35 years.

Empty.

But there seems to be a car there.

The motor has turned over.

A boat is
upside down.

Against a hedge
of currant bushes.

The cabins are one room
houses

laid out along the river
on a meter of land
on separate

tree trunks.

No light
almost.

Sky and grass
seen past tears

this is enough till death.

Sleep
does not help anymore
to understand God
with fingers.

Windows show
that History
holds promises of floods.

"Ma'am
let me introduce my self – your
husband was
once
mine.

I came a long
way to see
you and speak to you
about him –

the poor man
never thought
in all his life said
that suffering
is the only
experience.

Give it up,
I told him."

A woman is
or becomes
this trail.

A body sleeps
in a hallway

becomes
so miserable
and deadly.

Even when the cardboard box
in which
he spends the night

comes from a
packaging paradise

lost.

Survived
the man and so
the love –

for her not much time
left.

To take refuge
in her house.

The window has a religion
based entirely in localizing
the leaves of a tree.

After losing
everything

she gets ready
to expect
nothing.

Doors
closed.

Interrupted
conversations.

Windows
still display
what almost never moves
any
more.

The strength
not to take this book

but to open it

and read it.

And also to
write it

write a whole book
with no other
knowledge

than the flowers
and the trees –

Must one
continue to live
like this?

To change places
at night
with a blanket and a pillow

from the bed
to the couch?

On no one's couch.

She does not ask herself
if she gives
an impression
of devotion.

She lives without tenderness.

Alone.

Far from expected
physical

preoccupations.

The ladder
of spiritual evolution
insists
on the role
of saturated soil.

When a body
feels no more –
when a body
is ritual.

Desire
colors shadows –

she
in her chair

at nightfall

takes fright
at the silence

coming
off the river.

She just
interrupted herself

in the middle
of a sigh.

She hears –

someone walking
and crossing the bridge.

Goes away.

The uneasy softness

she finds it
in these passages.

The supreme humidity

that controlled by
the closed shutters.

Collars
hug

mistreat the neck.

She is attracted
by error and emptiness.

What can she
possibly expect
from her body?

There is no escape
from words.

Prisoner
of a wooden house

she doesn't move
any closer to the stove

listening
to her silence.

For hours
she looks at the grass

she is waiting for the resurrection
as if −

The enemy comes back.

Organs
vein
bodies.

This crack
in the ceiling

which she looks at
reading her newspaper

is a disaster or
a greeting.

A shawl is
over her shoulders
she thinks.

In the simple motion
of a day

the stream
is a mirror.

So far and so close
the world stays
elusive
to hand

to sight.

And the other bank
resolutely
strange.

She is. She enters
her house.

The light is
hers.

She creates
an obstacle system.

"I want
no more."

Tousled hair
this morning

how
to comb it?

Pulling
her hands through her
hair.

Between her fingers.

Her face
finds itself again

complies

with a Lutheran
prose.

The moon
is
still there

above the river.

The lit electric
bulb

gives off
a dull

silver glow.

She reads
intimating
an expression
of grief.

Her face
bears green
marks

on her
cheeks

just above
her lips formed
perfectly
by a deep dahlia
red.

Her eyes reply
to strangers
in the street.

She doesn't feel like dying.

She thinks about the death
of her family.

The shared heart.

Nothing is
more improvised.

From start to finish
life passes
for something else.

Frankly
what does she know?

What does she feel?

Reading.

Moving around the room.

She saves
what she can.

No doubt
first of all
the words.

The river's words.

Words
stung
by air – clean
as air.

Damp.

Full of
dampness.

Very.

Whatever the motion
of truth

she doesn't believe
her ears.

Because
since forever

all things are
before her

given.

From saucepan to
fork.

From bed to table.

She sucks her thumb
stirring the milk

in the bottom of the bowl
sour storm.

The lake is shown.

Words
are
shown

the undertaking
is
to go turn out the lamp

and find herself again
in the dark

with books
to read.

How many years
to be in love?

How much time
to be
disciplined

submitting
to the body?

Perhaps
to the word?

To want everything

poem and fate

in private –

Night. Under the covers.

Immensely
blonde –

in any case
enough
for one man.

Wherever.

She is not
wherever –

to wear cheap
dresses.

To live
amid
suitcases.

In the incompletion
of certain
structures.

Nothing ever
extra.

The air
lifts the house.

The wind
slaps the hulls.

All is lost
like a boat
gone down

in the midst of the waters
and lands.

It is said
in the Bible
there are many ways
to escape:

first of all
across the field.

Hull and wall
resound.

It's the same wall
where more than the truth
glides:

a fear – or its
vibration.

"I am in great
 danger."

The water is everywhere.

The great woods
are
everywhere.

No path. No direction.

Life spiraling.

Around a house
sitting on water.

Solitude

does she begin
with forgetting?

A whole life or
almost

in a cabin
at the waters' edge

is a picture
of a transitory defeat.

She does housework.

She washes
traces of skin.

Scours.

She rubs down
the sick

and scrubs their feet.

Soaps
the old folks

the tile work and

rinses.

She finds herself
before sickness
and death

that she does not examine according to urgency

but domestic necessity.

She does not stop herself from smiling.

She doesn't speak to any one. She doesn't know anyone anymore.

Wants
nothing.

A simple plan –

nothing more
to exact.

Suffer
day by day
insisting.

She has not to despair
for the human race

and even less
her body.

It fits –

it is child

it remains child –

the body.

Busier than ever
at being
emotion

in spite of the emptiness
all around.

Extreme
frailty

each time
sadness or joy
arises
in her eyes.

The scenery
suspended at the idea
of the disappearance
in the light

provokes
this double sense.

What tortures her
eats itself up

is thrifty
as the day.

But
possible

as
possible as
the release.

Who would come
here
and how?

In this place
old as the world
which exists
since forever?

Not a wall
to build
for a mason.

All the roofs
are tarred.

Each spring
the women hoisted onto the cabins

dunk their brooms
into pails

and strengthen
the roofs.

Cloths.
Pails and broomsticks

introduce ideas
of adultery and
murder.

The extreme solitude
delivers her
to an observance
of delinquency.

What does she know
of punishment?

Young woman
she scalded herself.

How?

Losing her balance

on a stool.

A frying
pan
spills oil

on the revealing breast

well she sees
she has been the victim
of a passion
of which she can't get free.

Black paths and
low branches.

Sparkling water
through the leaves.

Night announces
the hoodlum's caresses.

One is shoeless
the other shirtless.

He approaches
smelling of orange.

Evening
she drinks a glass of milk
and makes her eggs.

Her ear fills
with tears.

Horsehair mattress.

Such logic
can it still astonish

the Angel looking on

in silence?

She is
in a corner of the room.

Night is
falling.

Please
God
is not in her plan.

But
prevailing
on humility.

With this smile
of modest

abandon.

SECOND NOTEBOOK

"Sister Grace and Sister
Nettle

who are you
today?

My fear or my despair?

Deeper than
the lake.

Emptier
than my dress.

Sunday-
My-Humidity.

Earn all the rest.

Dinner devoured.

I have nothing left
in my pockets."

"Syllables
are eyes

then
I write

as a corpse
speaks
his sex-experience.

Abandoning
the idea
of entering a liaison

with
speaking
beings."

Is it
such a long journey

after having said
A

to decline
the whole alphabet

down to
Z?

How is it possible
to learn to love
one man

while loving another?

This moment of crisis
she rethinks it

at each instant
day and night.

She has done
for him
what no woman
has ever done
for anyone.

Her days pass
with that abyss
in her heart

before the white
river.

How is it possible
to learn to love one man

while loving
at the same time
her best friend?

A woman
asks herself this question.

Forty years
later.

The divine ease
of yesterday

disturbs
what she imagines
living
today

and the silence

she writes from
sometimes
the motions
toward the ear.

"There never has been
any sound
by the river."

She realizes
how much she is – wanting
to die –

exhausted

lost.

She rehearses for herself.

She plays
scenes in three for herself.

To not find herself again
alone
in the dark.

A green stream
runs

beneath the light in the woods.

"Whistle
and I'll come
running
like a dog."

Everything is
so moldy
and dark

as

a secret.

She always
smiles

in disorder

while buying
potatoes.

Her lips are
helpless.

The mountains are further away
than the storm

it arrives
above the funerary
excavations.

It's also
in the lit electric
bulb

where she watches
the desert
be unveiled
and the Ark

flowered with
blue chicory

her lips
bathed in honey and
maple
syrup.

In the evening
she covers a notebook
with slanted script

eating
angel
cake.

Call someone.

She is the one
who answers.

She is sitting
at the same table
as −

no one is there
but dishes
for several weeks.

Crumbs
on the floor

have the movements
of Exodus.

Tiny hands
offer
half the words

lines
follow and halo them
with dust.

Everything remains
in memory

like a
benediction.

Can she
at night again climb
the path of chaos
one last time?

The white portals
make arbitrary
separations.

Woods and fields
geometrical
according to –

the dream
begins to
stammer.

No
furniture No
tortured

sheen.

Beyond
the river –

the stammering genes amid
the duckweed.

Colored
according to the cloud
and death which pass.

Already late

even though
the extension –

the contract of
marriage
has
no date.

When she fastens
her necklace

on Sunday

with all the pearls
she has brought
comes
comfort.

She rubs
her two eyes
with her hands.

It is so late.

And waiting for
someone who's not coming.

Day breaks
beyond the curtains

flaming red.

What she wears
around her neck
is not an abstraction.

It is a familiar belief
she displays
and reheats in her hand.

Pearls are born
on a string

acquired
in the dream

where they blur
the score.

House moves
when she shakes the mattress

the hollow stamps itself
thus
in the bed turned over –

in the name
of weight
rather than a separation.

She talks to herself
with what she has.

She can't do without
language

and consulting with
the truth

which comes back to her
in the form
of a breached
conversation.

The man never belonged
to her.

Charm
does not leave
her face.

The real question is the following:
where are the men?

Her own feet
have no throne.

She wears no
robe –

and has nothing more
to dominate.

In exchange for dissolution
she looks for a country.

The river flows
between the days

from one shore to the other
with the night.

All the caresses are delivered.

Nature is a gland

sees trees grow

green.

Field all around –

it restores
the loving
ear.

She knows the river
nature

everything written.

The room
is the truth
against death.

Nothing
more can come near to
her books
but powder
                        dust
                                pollen

bacteria.

Why is the man coming
to shatter it?

Pins
to fasten
the colors of life
to a blanket

the child's
who sews with needle
heros and plants

ever nearer to
sleep.

When
it must
distract
her own feverish
hands.

The ear keeps the silence.

The sky is held back
without a syllable.

It's a scene of mirrors.

She fights
against fear

(testing to turn
the potatoes).

Her head down.

No one has a suspended
existence

as she.

What she knows and what she has seen –

dust
too

at the table
there where she is, writing

dust
too

and further
above

bound vault
penetrates
all the multitudes

the stars
too.

The white tablecloth
at lunch
is always an invitation
to the flood.

The stream floods
the plates.

Faltering life
sits there
with
its sighs

the experience
of words

always sitting
at
the table.

No need
to throw the dice

in the direction
of the river

they are heavier
than a dinghy.

Tears interrupt.

There.

And the page darkens.

She has some idea
of the infinite
every day and every night

when she goes
to get water
at the pump

in the middle
of the field

each stroke
splits and
paragraphs the pain

not
despair

but a grace
which grants

what is simplest
and fits the heart.

The life
unfolding here

between the stream
and the field

is it
somewhat

audible or
physical

like a
tide?

The word is written alone
is pronounced
"like a bride."

Improve
what is given

offered
by nature –

a place made
of four walls and a roof.

With door and
windows.

How to improve on
eternity?

With what
to begin?

"Someone
has to
die."

It's on the page
to say how

or in the book
to show where.

The time traveler
who stays sitting

looking at who comes
what grows

or blooms
studies this world

without clearing
its shipwrecked limits.

Her person
completes

in books
what she writes

a holiday
without audience
who kneeling

earns
filaments.

Unlawful world
and smiling which
changes her to rocks.

Why?

Because she lives in an unsettled
memory

a memory of property
and of the kingfisher.

Leaves
the pantry

to
refill

with elements
of emptiness.

Order takes into account
silence

and night.

There are the two resistances
and the two layers.

Midnight
and nothing –

dishes
drain

in a bucket.

To the attention
of no one

not even
regretting –

child of the holey saucepan
nature entire

as map

the infinite
can reach.

Sun setting
is a mourning.

Emphatic
mourning.

From her window
the world appears
on a stalk.

Sitting at her table
this world seems resting
on a pedestal.

Serving
sight.

Are planks
the definition
of the place
which drops there –

a house
thus hers happens to be
missing the sky

because a carpenter
transforms a surface
of beaten earth
into an attic paradise.

Coming back
but anticipating
the robin hidden in the tree

she bathes there the words

in this light
of crowned sighs

a sound whistles
near the basket

where she is putting
her shoes away
with a fistful
of wild berries.

A woman who
writes

often knows the art
of digging up
the potatoes.

She has to dig with one foot

lifting the clod
of earth

managing the root with one hand
while airing it out
and shaking it
against the shovel

grabbing with the other hand
so it won't roll away –

and starting over.

Before dying
she asks

that everything be burned.

Papers. Rugs. Letters.
Furniture.

Memories
burn
in the fields.

No one
objects
to this signature.

Daughter of farmers
rich in land
in farms in orchards

she is unaware that her father
is involved
for a lifetime
with a neighbor

farmer in her condition
to whom
he gives according to the opportunities

everything he owns
of fields and grassland.

Upon his death
she realizes

she has nothing but
a flooding meadow
with a raised cabin.

She moves in.

The thrones
are planks and floating
papers

vertical.

To receive
her hands.

Summer. Fall.

Snow and rain

the frosts are dynasties
naturally
enough.

Everything freezes
even the page promised to the world.

"Judge me!"

is
on that morning
fire
in the
snow.

Why?

Because
the judgment

will make plain
presences
of the resurrection.

It is not night

but a bell
she hears.

Forest and starry sky
bear the same world
known by books.

Put together
graves
        farms
                muscles.

An air all around.

And a sticker: "sex change" –

A woman who dreams
watches or suffers
while writing.

Does not standardize
a medicine

by means of the book
or its symptoms.

She draws
barely the traces
of a complaint
that would be called the garden

that yearns

desire that she is
by the river.

"No"
is a much more enormous
occasion that eats eyes.

To say "No."

"No"
of prayer –

"No"
of contemplation.

And its silence
as kind of
petal-wax –

"How to bear it?"

These river games
with moon and sun

never invent
the moment of an escape.

The chains
are at her feet

she sees
by what perfection
is affected

the great circumference
she calls
the hours.

The unknown
from the cabin

until her death
is at her washstand.

An extreme
occupation —

light bathes

absorbs the sand
of this sallow body

mysteriously
the tears.

A winter
draws or multiplies
the Ark
as far as the eye can see.

That year
the snow sweeps away
all the livestock
as far as the eye can see.

Space is empty.

White.

She discovers
in her cabin in a schoolchild's apron
what the word
"alphabet"
means.

The mosses all around
intervene and interfere
choke the sounds.

The drop of water

the step
      the pump.

And sense
is a hole
in the analogy.

There is nothing
to see
but an abstraction
of green light.

And some names:
blue chicory
      sweet cicely
            water flag.

Often
she speaks of forgetting
as a process of emptiness.

The paths
make sparks
in the woods

the play of branches
conveys the whites
that inhabit the dark.

Nature is thus
from a relief
literally bathed
by foggy light:

it hides
what is busy living
being born
             flowing away.

A simplicity
in life

in substance of life
damaging

rather than a
simple life.

Lamp lit beside her

that
the heart
does not bleed.

Tick –
tock

without visible or earthly machine.

A sound
closes
the year.

Awakening
in
parting.

Everything is
so
scrupulously –

book complete

flesh
complete.

The place
does not stop.

The river is always
in full
receipt.

A garden
lettuce

is no more within call
than the other bank

echoed about
by the walls
                by the bodies
by the books.

She
writes.

The shape of the chimney

also provides
a reassuring sight

(without

help)

from the roof −

perfect.

Smoke escapes
from a dream.

Enclosed
in a pod.

Snows and huge
farmers' wives

have the shyness
of love.

Covered up
even without motive.

Mightily drawn
in the sky

clouds pass
and form shadows
onto life.

The words have that same
airy machine
in the book.

Abstractions that
steer and fuse
their echoed
sense
to whiteness.

In all and
for all –

a house.

A book to write.

A cabin that watches the world
or a book already written.

How to write the other?

How and where to find
the words
with negative dimensions

to illuminate
the pages?

If the graves
are full of stripped nerves

the living
rouse them

and remember
their life.

Until when has she been
dressed
as a boy?

Irregular birth

is no
further
than behind
the cupboard.

Is she whole
in this space?

She comes in
alongside a fence.

She climbs
three steps.

The river is close by
the door

she is opening.

Memory
eases the work of reading.

Memory awake or active
helps differentiate –

to reverse
the content

of the wounded speech –

how to learn to live
the wound in reverse?

It is the equivalent of the big storm.

Full sky
in open perspective.

The gable of the barns
has the shape
of a Dutch
dean's cap

or a lace-maker

one promised to Christ

along the way.

Bells far off and murmurs
of hallelujah
in the huge expanse

clearly
a convent
takes shape there

in the kingdom of the river.

A woman
is turning pages backwards.

Waterlogged soil
and toxic

close to the black filth.

Mouths that decompose

imprisonment is
revelation

before the sky so familiarly
blue.

No day
without day.

Opposite.

Eternity at the window
dies
too
behind the curtains.

Do
not deny
the grave.

Stirs
a nerve
inside her

that she strips
and swallows

to go to sleep
according to the old custom
of mortals.

There is a little girl

who was able to grow up
to the size of the book
like a doll

in the snow
                    in winter

in the field of feathers

during several lives.

THIRD NOTEBOOK

White moon

                Scullery moon

above the river

that it bathes and floods.

There is a continent that dives.
The house is tilted.

A woman mends.

She says
that she feels lost.

What are hours
and a day
after hours?

She does housework and
the washing.

At the hospital she bathes
the dead and dying.

She sews aprons.

She comes home sometimes with a pail
of dandelions or
a bag of snails.

Always the foothold

the body held
by the ropes.

The dinghies fastened.

The women fastened-moored.

She spent her life

on nothing.

A whole existence
waiting in water.

Waiting

for the water not to rise any more.

A whole existence
waiting

in the mud.

Duck feathers
among the horsetails

what she sees
while walking
toward the upside-down dinghy

release the impulses.

Indian memory
still journeys
the length of the peninsula.

Who sings
and sometimes cries
in silence?

A woman
hears an unnatural
sound.

She waits for the flood
that does not come.

She waits for the ice
and winter.

The snow that does not come.

Idea of returning
to origins.

She hides out with a man
in the closet.

She does not live
buried.

Vital motion
is simple

it goes
from possession to dispossession

and to repossession.

There is a very ancient
storm

above
the flooded grave.

Water green and tender green
at the bottom of the pond

without origin
or clear message.

The excavation is flooded.

The house is flooded.

The earth is missing.

There is even a wearing away

for all is marsh
gorse
and mud

with huts at the horizon
no surface.

Midges form a cartilage
on everything they displace:

phantom-tarragon.

The kisses
from the marsh

she brings them
to her lips

chapped
icy.

Who does she need?

No one.

For it's a question of hiring her labor

or letting her slide into the mud.

How to oppose
real estate
farming
and hiring of labor?

How
and why not?

How
not to think:

speech
       writing
              language –

For whom

for those who
remain alive?

Sometimes she camps out
in the bush

without breathing

without catching
a single carp.

Writing
is what keeps her outside the emptiness.

Checkered shirt
red and green
with black stripes

buttoned up to the neck.

Define: earth
ooze
mud.

Isolate the earth
like — an embryo.

Three long noises
sudden
by the shore.

Is silence
accustomed to the noise
of time
flowing by?

She did not even want
to pick up a plate
or
hold a spoon.

Before dying
she forbid herself

from changing
anything at all.

Child
of
thunder –

no more sight.

White
as sugar – salt or snow –

in touch
with stolen horses

spirit
reckons
incantations.

Warrior herbalist

she sews
the larch leaf
to the first page.

Begins the Book.

Brothers
of the wind

speak to the horses.

The spirits
the stories
welcome the child.

A blackbird
is whistling
in the marsh.

The last Indians
still whistle
in their bones.

The length of the marsh
along the peninsula.

They immerse air

give life
to the ooze.

They dig pits
in the earth

that they brace
with pruned
branches –

what plants
do they cultivate

for spirits or
for wounds?

The cemeteries keep
room for coyotes and
chamomile flowers.

In view
of the flooded fields

eyes
with long lashes
have the freshness of cellulose.

Feathered
dolls

watch.

This place is hers.

She comes back to this place
each time
writing –

if she is and
who she is

without ever recovering
anything
from this earth

or hiding a place
of why
where
how

"I am not in my place."

She happens
to swim
out of the water
around the house.

There is really a swimming motion
in her arms and legs.

She glides
and floats on the ground and
moves
as though on a board
fixed to ball bearings.

This does not remain
forever.

Night

outside her door is
where rodents
come
to taste the eggs.

All outside.

She has found the world
again.

She finds
each thing.

She is busy putting
stones back
to distract her thoughts.

Dissolving certainty
in the ordinary –

she is compelled
simply to look.

The whole
body against
the absurd.

She lets
her body
see −

the description
glides

that winds
around
her wrists.

Amazing bride at
sixty years old

she remarries
a phantom neighbor
who knocks one beautiful morning
at her door:

"Who are you?"

She is odd
and he will see in not much
time

how much in fact
she is.

She takes
to the path
of return.

She loses the place.

She will never again find
the place.

She leaves.

The river
                the garden
                                the house
remain.

Leaning.

And her evergreen.

All meaning
stands for:

a foreseeable disappearance
includes
the proof of all relationship.

A woman is life.

The noises
that haunt
the woods

appear
like a masked speech.

They
transform this woman
in person

because she recognizes
the whistle call.

A system
that uses a wall
she calls "addressee."

Stick hits the air. Stones
hit the air. Tapping a foot.

All this arouses
a great wind.

Stricken language
changes place
with the almost silent echo.

Outside the door
of her house

she leaves at night
a pot
full
of strange stew

prepared
with honey and chestnuts.

With seashells

or goose carcass.

Nature
thus becomes known

expresses in metaphor
its office.

The woman cooks the last Friday
of every month

in a granite pail
all kinds of books
mixed with flour

that she eats
on the river bank.

She eats books
at home too

and no one
surprises her in the tub.

For
she always
gives the appearance of a woman perfectly
dressed

with eyes
of normal life.

In the large pot
is a package of peel
regressive nourishment
of thought

for Lent.

This woman
with the red checked blouse

got rid of
the woman

after evisceration.

She is calm
leaning against the evergreen.

With the smile
as calm
as a spoonful of wild fruit.

Certain texts affirm
that otters
ask and teach

have a language

they cross the river
of booms
            currents and
sounds.

Women have always agreed
to give themselves to otters

in exchange for the promise
of being more able to fish for carp
than men.

Today they look at
otters going
downstream

opening shells
on their stomachs.

The stream flowing in the woods
serves as a resonator

and crying near the river
fills a whole program
of melodic phrases.

Laments are musical
instruments

and the evergreens
troughs
bursting with sap
and women
in tears.

The length of clothesline
creates a humming
from the commotion of sheets.

Morning announces itself
with the wind.

Where do the rattles
shake?

Bank side or laundry side?

That must be covered in leaves.

Above the sky.

With the lightness of water.

Without forgetting the first steps
in the mud.

Susceptible to smell
and intolerant of any stain

she – always
imparts a childishness to
her simple life

at the bottom of the pot
a kind of love she eases

she herself eases
talks of the next book

bears witness to history
as ancient
as the vulnerability
of the sea-slug and the sea-
otter.

Still the same trees
standing

they lean
in the water

looking for boats

in the hollow trunks
filled with water.

She always
smiled
at any charge.

That
is not
really
a life of silence.

The body
is never
silent.

A last
vision of her:

she begins to whistle
lining things up
on the shelves

straight
in front of the field.

AFTERWORD: Mirrors, Reflections

Imagine my astonishment—a letter is on the floor. Not stamped, so someone has dropped it in the mail slot by the blue door.* The return address is a hotel in San Francisco. I open the envelope carefully. Out of it falls a letter written in blue-black ink, in someone's inimitable handwriting. It is Jean Daive. Jean Daive! What, here, in San Francisco? No, was here, and now gone. "De passage dans votre ville." He can't resist, he says, giving me these pages, xeroxes of Lorine Niedecker's letter to Cid Corman about her astonished reading of Daive's *White Decimal*, "nothing new matters after the Daive" etc. And now, 40 years later, he inhabits and interprets her astonishment, her interrogations, and writes a book of poems in relation, *Une femme de quelques vies*. He'd like me to translate this book.

But first we must go back to his writing of *Décimale blanche*. As Jean Daive writes in an email, "I'll recap the story for you:

> "Existence of *Décimale blanche* with almost simultaneous readings of Paul Celan, André du Bouchet, Louis-René des Forêts, Jacques Dupin, Yves Bonnefoy.
>
> First publication in *l'Ephémère numéro 2*. [journal]
>
> Immediate publication in *Mercure de France* in 1967. [book]
>
> Immediate translation by Cid Corman in his journal *Origin*.

With this remark from André du Bouchet: "Are you aware Jean Daive that a man who lives at the other end of the world is translating you? Cid Corman just told me so."

"Appearance of *Origin 13* which reaches Lorine Niedecker in her Wisconsin solitude.

Lorine Niedecker has *Origin 13* sent to Louis Zukofsky.

Taking a walk with CRJ [Claude Royet-Journoud] he tells me that in her correspondence Lorine Niedecker has written about her reading *Décimale blanche*. ["*Between Your House and Mine*": *The Letters of Lorine Niedecker to Cid Corman, 1960 to 1970.* Ed. Lisa Pater Faranda. Durham, NC: Duke UP, 1986]

"More than twenty years later, I go to Lorine Niedecker's small town in search of the river and the famous 'cabin.'

I then write *A Woman with Several Lives.* You, Norma Cole, translate this book, appropriating Lorine Niedecker's vocabulary.

A vrai dire, tout cela donne le vertige."

*which Jean Daive refers to as "la porte rose." When I meet him in Paris, he tells me his address, "la porte rouge."

Author of over fifteen collections of poetry and seven volumes of fiction, Jean Daive has been an important voice in French letters for over 35 years. His first publication, *Décimale blanche*, which came out in 1967, received much attention; his subsequent volumes have often been serial—*Narration d'équilibre, Trilogie du temps, La Condition d'infini*, each exploring a specific concept and/or formal question across three or more volumes. His work has received extensive critical attention, both in full-length volumes and numerous articles. Also a translator, he has published translations of Celan and Creeley, among others. Daive has also exerted a great influence through his decades of work in radio as a producer at *France Culture*, as president of the centre international de poésie *Marseille* (le cipM), and as the founder and editor of three successive poetry journals, *Fragment* in 1969, *fig.* in 1989, and *Fin* in 1999. He lives and works in Paris.

Norma Cole, born and raised in Canada, has been involved with contemporary French poetry since the late '60s. In addition to volumes of poetry by Anne Portugal, Danielle Collobert, Fouad Gabriel Naffah, and Emmanuel Hocquard, she has translated a volume of critical work, *Crosscut Universe* (Burning Deck, 2000) and a book of interviews with Jean Daive. A student at New College of California in the '80s and a close associate of Robert Duncan's, Cole has published over ten volumes of poetry, including a selected, *Where Shadows Will* (City Lights, 2009). Cole began her life as a visual artist, an experience that has informed her several cross-media projects, from a CD-rom, *SCOUT,* (Krupskaya, 2004) to her much-vaunted four-month installation *Collective Memory*, which took the rich history of poetry and visual arts in the San Francisco Bay Area as its launching point (California Historical Society, 2004–2005). A collection of essays and talks, *To Be At Music,* was published by Omnidawn in 2010. She lives and works in San Francisco.

This is the eighth title in the La Presse series of contemporary French poetry in translation. The series is edited by Cole Swensen and designed by Shari DeGraw. This book is set in Interstate, designed by Tobias Frere-Jones.